The Razor of Your Smile

Anthony Xavier Jackson

*This collection of poetry is dedicated
To my father, Wardell Jackson.*

You always encouraged me to continue to write, even when it did not make sense to me.

Published by Anthony Xavier Jackson.

Melanin Productions, 2025.

The Razor of Your Smile

Edited by Zarmineh Zarouhi.

First edition. February 2025.

Copyright © 2025. Anthony Xavier Jackson.

All rights reserved. Neither this book, nor any parts within it, may be sold or reproduced in any form without permission.

ISBN: 979-8-9919373-2-0

Acknowledgements

My gratitude to the editors of the following journals, magazines and podcasts in which these poems first appeared, sometimes in previous iterations:

Bloody Mary, BARBAR
Sweat Anthology

Liquid Diamonds, The Word's Faire
The Feast Anthology

Imposter, Quillkeepers Press TAP Journal, Q2 2024

Potter's Grave, Wingless Dreamer
The Silver Lining of Heartbreak Poetry Contest, 2024

Embers and **Black**, Dipity
Whisker Factory

Breakfast In Bed, Wingless Dreamer
Dreamscapes and Daydreams Poetry Contest, 2024

Arrogancia, Wingless Dreamer
Petals and Pines Poetry Contest, 2024

Say Their Names, *new words press*
New Words, Issue #4

Trauma*, The Stardust Review*

The Razor of Your Smile, *Creation Magazine*

Bertha*, Poetry Society of New Hampshire Touchstone, Volume 66*

Fentanyl*, Willowdown Books*

Making Babies*, God's Cruel Joke Literary Magazine*

Famine, *Tule Review, 2024*

Introduction

This collection of poetry has been organized into five sections; allow me to explain them.

Seditious Sobriety: These poems are basically about the rebellion my mind underwent in the process of not only getting, but remaining sober from all substance use starting 10 years ago. I think abstinence for me has been like an insurrection of all my expectations, emotionally and spiritually. It is my hope that these poems capture the raw truth of addiction and some of the light at the end of that seemingly endless tunnel. Sobriety is seditious.

Trauma Bonded: These are poems mostly about my father and the time I got to spend with him before he succumbed to cancer. The 23 Psalms series of poems are intended as conversations between the two of us following him losing the ability to use his deep, dark, and beautiful voice. At his funeral, I read the 23rd Psalm, which has always been very special to me - probably the passage that planted the seed in me to write poetry in the first place…go figure!!!

The House Where Tornadoes Live: These poems are reflections on my childhood mostly, but amount to a wild roller coaster ride of themes and emotions that I hope will raise goosebumps on the inside of your skulls.

Love Is Political: Because it is, as a Black Queer Man in America, nothing could be more true. Everything we do, especially our love, is political, there's just no getting around that. Even our own self destruction is political. I've never been good at political poetry until I accepted the fact that my whole existence is just that, political. Who I kiss, who I don't, where I sleep and who I love fiercely…all political from day one.

A Speculative Future Past: I have always deeply admired speculative fiction thanks to Octavia Butler and the likes of mavericks like William Burroughs. These poems venture into the uncomfortably all too familiar speculative future
where it could all be a fever dream, or one day bear haunting resemblance to days yet to come. This is what I do best, daydreaming with a tinge of Revelations thrown in.

You will notice some poems written by Embers the Cat, who is my writing alter ego, and literally, my old cat. I would channel her words, or at least that is what I told myself. I am honored to bring her words to the world. I want to thank my editor, Zarmineh Zarouhi, for her endless patience and very precise editing of all my wayward punctuation and outright and outlandish embellishments.

I want to thank GTFO Poetry Collective - Kay Miller, Al Cortez, and Anthony Robles, for allowing me to be a part of this incredible group of writers.

I want to thank the many poets I got to workshop with, whipping many of the published pieces into superior shape.

There are so many kind souls in Sacramento who have helped me since I first showed up on Luna's stage years ago: Jenny and Sho' Nuff Davidson, Art Luna, Patrick Grizzell, Professor Andy Jones, Susan Kelly-Dewitt, Escritores del Nuevo Sol, Sacramento Poets Society, Andru Defeye, Laura Phillips, Christina Jackson, Jeanette Rowe, Terry Moore, Brickhouse Open Mic, Michael Gallowglas, Anna Marie and Poetic Butterfly. I am sure I could not name everyone who has showered me with love in this city. I especially want to thank Diamond

Key for inviting me out to Luna's to perform. This is where my journey as a Sacramento poet began.

But, I have been doing poetry for a long time, since the mid 90's in San Francisco's Lower Haight, which is where I got my start as a performer, producer and host of open mics. I want to thank Zahra Selah, who owns Café International, for letting me grow and develop this love of the stage. I hosted a weekly open mic there for nearly a year. I also would not be anywhere near the poet I am today without having met the incredible and one-of-a-kind Royal Kent and his project Copus. I was able to organize the first shows for Copus at Arena Interplay. We did quite a few showcases of fellow poets, like Chani Di Prima and Dee Russell, to name a few.

These words of his will always guide me:

"What must be conveyed here is greater than what can come from only pen and ink.
Those of us tripping in Trip City, walking a crooked path straighter than you think. Only two things to be said here, it's later than you think, later than you think…" - Royal Kent, *Later Than You Think*

Last, but not least, I want to thank Author D. Scot Miller for the line from one of his poems, "Let your smile be your razor…" It inspired the title of this book. Thanks to our writing group, Blackbard, for planting the seed. Thanks to you all for watching it grow!!!

Table of Contents

Section One

Seditious Sobriety

Liquid Diamonds	2
Potter's Grave	4
Making Babies	5
Fentanyl	7
Ada Fia*	9
Home	12
Astral Levity*	14
Sober	18
Safe Travels	22
The Harmless*	24
Dysthymia	26
Home Sweet Homeless	29
Embers	32

Section Two

Trauma Bonded

23 Psalms 1 – Welcome Goodbye	35
The Falling Sky	38
The Razor of Your Smile	41
Famine	44
Imposter	47
23 Psalms 5 - Church and State	49
23 Psalms 6 - Black Male American	51
23 Psalms 9 – Catgut Jazz	54
Grief	56
To My Son	60
Breathe	63
Promises	65

Section Three

The House Where Tornadoes Lived

Trauma	70
Bloody Mary	72
Richelle	75
Arrogancia	77
Rabies	79
Restraint	81
Lost	83
Black*	86
Music Theory 2- The Minor Chord	87
Collapse	94
Duality	96
Trauma 3- The Ghost	98

Section Four

Love is Political

Say their Names	104
Bertha	108
Babylon Chant	111
Breakfast in Bed	114
Labyrinth	116
Buzzards Bay	118
Thee Psychick President	119
Covid	121
The Avenging Angel of Election Year	123
The National Anthem	125
Breathless	127
Love is Revolutionary	129
Short All-Purpose Love Poem	132

Section Five

A Speculative Future Past

Religion	134
Famous (with an F flat)	136
Open Mic	138
Visceral Incorporated	141
A Little to the left	144
September 23, 2035	148
The Moon Retreats	153
The Robot Wars	156
Burnout	159
Peanuts	161
Babylon	162
10 Things I Know	164

Poems written by Embers the Cat

Section One

Seditious Sobriety

Liquid Diamonds

On my moon
You spell incorrectly
You conjure up dragons
When you wanted butterfly sprees

On this plane
The silver thread that
Holds you to your body
Snaps at the merest hint
Of chaos, shaking
The chassis whenever anyone
Looks at you funny

I scratched your surface
Found liquid diamonds
Bubbling beneath your
Thick skin
For all the potential value
Within the folds of you
There was no story
Quite as lucrative
As when the self-love began

You're
Cyanide eyeshadow
Heavy metal pout pillow
Sunset shaded palpitations on a
Shredded planet
Which rains sulfur when

The violent evenings coalesce
In this sieve
Of reality
With a bariatric sleeve
We're pouring
Liquid diamonds in

Until the light under your dying eyes retreats

Until the shadow eclipsing your bloom
leaves

Until the quasar of your greatest fear
collapses

Until you are rocked to sleep
By the curses of your ancestors
Curling away stoically in the flames of
Parnassus.

Potter's Grave

Bring to me
Your tattered
Your unborn
Your unclaimed
Wrapped in Muslin Cloth
Left bloated out in the rain.

Bring to me
Your homeless unnamed
Laid naked next to the tracks
Where the foster children
Of casual psychopaths
Throw rocks at police cars
Right before they are swept off
In anonymous white panel vans.

Bring to me
Your beloved sons
Faces torn by war
Whose limbs twist
Splayed
In a mockery of valor
Turned black like my tongue
Wrapping around this turbulent song
Which strangers burying strangers
Becomes.

Making Babies

Everything is prayer
With your
Soft
Magnificent
Inviting
Hopeful
Downy warm
Drowsy
Eyes wide open

We're supine
Hot
Skin
On skin
Soliciting
The heaven
Between
Curled lips
Praying
To drip celestial babies
Into doubts
Eclipsed

Swallowing the shape
Swaddled in the warmth
Of my teeming tongue
The kaleidoscope you are
Eats corners
Blisters suns

Churns smooth
7-year itches
Into calm lion hums

Do you think
When
Our ancestors
Watch us play
They place bets
On which stars
Our explosions will burn
Today?

Fentanyl

There's a cold
Spray of Narcan
Up my nose
I come to fighting
Screaming for more
More of what kills me
Feeling like
A glitchy cartoon
On a fuzzy TV screen

Coping is inevitable
Is the commercial
They sell me
I avoid mirrors
There are sores
I never want to see

Fetty
Feel so good
I'm feeling nothing at all

Everyone's eyes are mirrors
Reflecting my scars
Where can I get more?

The EMTs tell me I was flatlined
Second time this week, blue,
Talking to an old boot
I couldn't hear you

Jaw felt like a bone saw
Rugged, rigid, raw

I only want more
More of nothing at all

Maybe next time the Batch won't put me
Corpse stiff
On the corner
Leaned over myself
Skull
Scratching at the floor

In this tender oblivion
The slam of ambulance doors becomes
All too familiar

You good
They ask me
I'm
Feeling nothing at all
I float away sick
To more
More of what kills me
Fentanyl.

Ada Fia

Ada Fia goes jogging
Down the Great Highway
In a pair of orange underwear
Stolen from 850 Bryant
Holding a sign saying rob me
While carrying a rusted saxophone
That he can be seen cavorting in
The sea raging with lunacy like
Clockwork every evening at 8:34
He clamors to the shore in those skivvies
To recite poetry and honk out obscene
Morose echoes of possibly once known
Sanity
The rangers just watch as he exits the water
Goes jogging back to his hovel behind the
San Francisco Zoo
No one has ever robbed him

Ada Fia
Likes every now and then to go buy a cheap
New wallet and leave his old one with a two
Dollar bill sitting on the sidewalk of Mission
And Sixth, where he sits on the steps of the
US Mint with his phone filming
The ensuing skepticism of all the people
who walk by it as if it were a wounded dog
trying to

Speak English, to explain in plaintive tones it has some intrinsic value, that it's ok to touch...
Eventually a homeless person reaches down and smiles as they pocket the two-dollar bill. Ada Fia has a whole YouTube channel filled with little movies of people avoiding the wallet until one brave soul dares.

Ada Fia likes to glue an especially rare coin to the sidewalk outside of Sotheby's door and watch as the well-coiffed collectors try and try futilely to remove it, each looking about over their shoulders like a runaway slave trying to make sure they aren't being watched. Ada Fia has taken the time to formulate a unique epoxy that only he has the solvent for and every time
At exactly 8:34am he removes the coin and posts his videos while having a nice cup of cocoa wrapped up in his foil blanket.

Ada Fia is later seen enjoying a makeshift plate of goodies hijacked from the Rainbow Grocery dumpster for which he has a key. Ada Fia is vegan, but loves to go to Animal Republic in Berkeley and talk to all the passersby about the benefits of cannibalism, says we shouldn't put our chemical laden bodies into the earth in corrosion proof boxes. Ada Fia argues with all the DXE

head honchos about the efficacy of animal liberation, and can be seen outside the Butcher's Son Delicatessen waving a placard that says "If God didn't want us to eat people, then why are they made out of meat?"
Ada Fia is many things, but among them you may never count him as bored...
Ada Fia protests the long running Goth club using a lynched man as a logo and all the powdered white patrons ignore him and pass a mirror between themselves fecklessly
Ada Fia can't decide what pronoun to use
Ada Fia says everything tastes like chicken
Chicken Chicken
Psycho Chicken Pot Pie
Chicken Adobo in a Dojo with a Dobro
And a portrait of Nancy Reagan not crying
At Ronnie's funeral.
Ada Fia tries every day to sneak a camera into the courtrooms of various counties, where he records random dialogue and cuts it up to play as a lullaby for the tigers who have learned to just ignore the funny man in orange underwear who lives in a hovel

Behind The San Francisco Zoo.

Home

The bones are good
I've lived here my whole life
I would not sell it
Though I might rent you
A quiet space
Down by the river

Where the expectation
That anyone's opinion
Will heal me
Sits quietly in a tent
Huffing superglue

Where my mother's love
Is reflected in your eyes
Root beer amber
Elusive eyes
Lapping at the shore
We walk without a word

Reminding me
To let the dog in
He chases squirrels
Until his feet bleed

Reminding me
I've lived here my whole life
You can come in
But take off your shoes

Leave the sedatives
At the door
Leave the right words
At the foot of the bed

I might just turn
The air conditioner on.

If you're extra good
I'll let you see
My smile
Becomes a futon
That comforts
Alcoholic ailing Aunts
Morose Molotov Memories
Titillating twisting tsunamis
Newborn mawkish maybes
Tornado alley
Depression dishes
Feeding patchwork
Mismatched families

The bones are good
You can lean on them
I've lived here my whole life
Despite my best harsh efforts
The frame is not rotten

Come on in…

The kettle is singing.

Astral Levity
By Embers the Cat

We are in the Lower Haight
Actually, I am laying on my human's
Bed next to a beautiful woman who speaks
to me
In her lilting voice, who calls me kitty
She tries to get me to bite her hand
She's silly

I digress
I am poised in spirit on the shoulders of my
human

In astral levity

We are dining at Cafe International
Where he used to work 20 odd years ago
Long before I was born
There is a group of disgruntled tenants
Meeting with a recalcitrant building owner
There is an exchange of terse words
Taciturn
As voices lower to growls
Cheap cigarettes and resentments burn

I do not understand this game at all.

20 years later, the café owner has grey hair

There is still the same guy who talks to
EVERYONE walking around looking like a
stoned Jesus. He compliments us on our
Purple Rain Tee shirt and stares blankly
At us eating while drunks talk to their dogs
outside of Molotov's bar. It seems the dogs
want to go next door where the smell of
charred pork emanates, hypnotizing them...

This game I understand

Poised on the shoulder of my familiar
My human.

He carries a guitar case down the street
Eyes searching the buildings for emaciated
memories
City Ghosts in unwritten lyrics

As the Jesus man fades to black
A trio of ethanol laden angry men pass
around
A bottle in a paper bag, the sun sets
On us all
Rich
Poor
Stoned
Dead
Sober
Enthralled

I tell my
Familiar to come home
Away from this weary city
Where you can hear the ennui
In the drawling voices of strangers
Who breathe the same pork heavy air of
Regrets like starving children
Who can only stare

We finish our tea
We quaff some tahini
We ignore the fact
We're in a place

No one remembers anyone
A place we don't belong

So, we paint humans on a wall
Every shade
Every iteration
A veritable mandala

To remind the customers
They're not alone

To comfort them
To soothe disgruntled tenants
To remind them to blend
The acidity of coffee
With the illusory smoothness
Of American Spirits

In a place where Jesus Man
Won't stop talking to strangers
While he's wandering

I ride on the shoulders of

My human
My familiar

My
Fallen star
Whose
Tears never flow
I purr to him
Hurry home.

Sober

I love watching

Drunk people

Dance

With 22 dollar

Multicolored

Drinks in their

Flailing hands

And the band played on

I won't give you

A cigarette

But you can

Certainly sleep

In my bed

Feed the cat

That lives in my brain

Clap along in off time

Because oft-time

I'm silent

I'm just waiting for you

To fall apart

To fall right into my arms

The lights

The lights

Make me dizzy

I ask

What's your one vice?

But I can't hear your voice

Over the bassline

You tell me I'm beautifully flawed

I'll never disagree

But tonight

I cannot dance

Can't you see how

The bartender slaps

My hand when I try to leave

A ten-dollar tip

For a five-dollar drink

With the funds

I stole from a chef

Who always lets me eat for free

On Saturdays

The moon is almost full

You seem really nice

Like psychedelics

In a broke down van

Over by the dirty river

Where parents warn

Their kids to never go

But I'll go with you

I'll go with you

I'll just watch you misstep

When it's time to reel

The stardust in

The last call bell ringing

I'll just watch

You slip on

your sideways grin

22-dollar drink

In your flailing hands

And the band played on…

Safe Travels

Maybe along the way
I'll see you again
Strolling in your underwear
Past the spots we used to lay
Cold barren stares
On the sidewalks
Looking for cigarette butts

Maybe along the way
You'll recognize my change
As I try to find your soul
In eyes long ago burnt
Down to the nub
Where the welfare check
Won't assure your sanity
Won't feed your cub
Does not pay for the eye
Of the needle where camels
Dance all night
To cheap European dubs.

Maybe along the way
All the humming of fentanyl smiles
Will disappear into tenderloin alleys
Where nothing matters but death's
Cool menthol flavored last breath
Where the last words we uttered
Are stuttered by an inconvenient
Service dog

You've taught to beg for meth
But never for change

Change that never lands
Change that taxis the runway
Pleading forever
For a place to blend
Blowing smoke rings while
The shock of contact
Numbs the stroke victim's hand.

The Harmless
By Embers the Cat

It's all the things you don't
Know you need
Not necessarily the smell
Of rotting pee on these streets

But the way it reminds us
That death
Impending
Lustful
Greedy
Indifferent
Spitting at us
Holding a can for donations
Propelled by need

Never Sleeps

Sit in this car
A broken table lamp on the bonnet
Sit in this car
Pretend no one can see us
Sit in this car
Smoke this shit
Pretend we are different
That we don't care

It's not even the smell of cheap dope
Permeating the hopeless air

That matters

It's just the way it reminds us

Death

Never

Sleeps

Death

Never

Sleeps

But neither can we.

Dysthymia

You told me everything was alright
Like you were never actually broken
You held your head up real high
On a swivel of disappointment and pride
I asked how are you dear friend
I'm fine you insisted
But more untrue words
Were ever spoken
So, sing to me sweetly
While upon your own bile
You're choking

How does it feel to feel nothing at all?
How does it feel to jump but never actually fall?
If you tell me your story, I can write it on all the walls
Until the Day Glo vermin open up
Their very own super mall
Where Dysthymia can be found reserved on sale
Two for one I hear tell
With a special promotional offer of a ride
That takes you straight to Hell

When I look deep in your eyes
You beg me please stop
When I hug you shiver
Though you insist it doesn't hurt a lot

When I say hey you seem down
You convince me that you're on top
While the commercial of calm contentment
Plays I shake my tiny fist at the box
The box doesn't care
The box has no thoughts
The box can never feel me
When I skulk about
In the dark
The box that your heart's in
Rumbles until you can't talk
But pack it all in stoically dear
Until the throbbing stops

How does it feel to feel nothing at all…

Given the option
I'd weave you into my special loom
Where the dark creatures
In the night moss can no longer
Sneak in your room
Where the dour voices of anhedonia no longer
Cast their spells convincing you
Like the radioactive rodent salesmen
That the joy you feel couldn't possibly be true

How does it feel when nothing belongs to you?

How does it feel to jump but never actually
pull your chute?
If you tell me your story, I can write it on all
the walls
Until the Day Glo vermin open up
Their very own super mall
Where Dysthymia can be found reserved on
sale
Two for one I hear tell
With a special promotional offer of a ride
That takes you straight to Hell.

How does it feel to feel nothing at all…

Home Sweet Homeless

Harmless…That's what I tell the cops
This glass pipe and acetylene torch
They aren't harming anyone but me.

The cops laugh bored, uncomfortably
As they drag me kicking and screaming
In my underwear out from underneath the
burning I beams of the squatted warehouse
myself and my ten best imaginary friends
live in

We all gather around a coffin
Perched precariously on milk crates
in the middle of the floor
No one has any clue where it came from
We burn the insulation from copper wire
around it
Pretending we're conjuring demons

While the rats fight each other for crumbs of
meth
We place bets on which one of the neurotic
pit bulls we keep as pets will be the first
attacked by the warped rodents who defy
every form of poison we can concoct
Chewing with lackluster grins through the
buckets of barbeque scraps laced with
arsenic.

Running water and electricity used to be free in the squat
Until we discovered we could make money by stripping the wire and pipes, smoking it right up in the dark waiting for the stolen generator fumes to knock us out.

But it's harmless, I tell the cops as the flames spread to the coffin, dangerously close to the tank of oxygen that had been used by the old man who came to stay last month who just as suddenly stopped breathing. They tell me a hot shot got him and Daphne is still collecting his SSI check. They rolled him up in a carpet and left him next to the Best Buy Dumpster last week with the needle still in his neck.

I persuaded my girlfriend to come back with a pack of generic cigarettes, she's been hanging out with Rico again in that broken-down van and I guess he ran out of dope for her to slam. She's back and forth like my concept of self-worth. Rico says he never touches her, but I know everyone else there does, all it takes is a push of the syringe to make her dance. She reminds me of my mother, she hates my poetry, she steals, she always leaves, hands in her back pockets, asking for money.
She's home sweet homeless

But always comes back to me
Though I know she died a year ago
It's harmless I tell the cops
If I steal enough copper
She'll finally make love to me.

Embers

Lately my cat looks
Disdainfully on me
Asking irritatedly

What's wrong with your damn stripes, kitten

You smell like desperation
Tinged untamed anxieties
Fears dancing with serotonin depletions
To symphonies of prefrontal deletion
Where the cavemen all too familiar
Beats on a drum skinned with lost ambitions

You didn't know my cat could speak
My cat she's a writer

My cat probably has her own TV show
In a parallel universe

My cat is a pride mother
Constantly telling me

Let that shit go.

She licks my forehead as if the grief
Can be removed by that spiky pink tongue
She bites my toes as if my fears hide there
If only she could torture the right one.
She gets high on catnip and sips

At my tears in the flurry of my dreams
When I wake between dimensions she's
speaking

What's wrong with you kitten
In sadness you're soaking
What's wrong with you kitten
What work related burden are you hugging
What's wrong with you kitten
Your astral pants are sagging
What's wrong with you kitten
Your fur is laced with the dandruff
Of stressing

I don't know what to tell her
I just know I can hear her
In the darkness

Always
Prowling

Inquiring

Section Two

Trauma Bonded

23 Psalms 1 – Welcome Goodbye

Welcome
I just wanted to say
Relax
Have a seat right there
Breathe
Tell me the highs and lows
Sigh
Bear the weight of a feather
Upon this scale which measures

Your heart
Tell me all the things you remember
Your mind
A fascinating theme park
Glowing
With the last embers of epic
Light eating dark
Waters
Poured before the feet of Gods
Who do not stalk
Cherubim who do not talk
Ancestors who upon our shoulders

Walk

Walk with me a little while
In the gossamer Susurrus
My dreams make your limbs
Whole again, my dreams

Make your baritone boom again,
My dreams tattoo your disappearance onto precise
Nerve clusters that sing pain
Painting an incisive pidgin English
Portrait of ironic freedom
In the sunsets of Bossier Parish
The flash floods of Little Rock
The horseshoe
Nebulas in the triceps of generations
Of toiling trapped men

Put your chest to my ear
So I can hear Granny talk
Put your hand once more
Atop my tiny Afro so I can feel
The impact of a metric ton
Of cotton in those splendid fingers
Waving back and forth to
My gray hairs

Welcome
You tell me
Relax
Sit yourself down
Breathe
You should drink some water
Tell me about it

Write

Until your heart
Is the weight of the drop
Of water that turns a storm
To flood

The Falling Sky

There are days that come
Knocking on my door

Days that I'm responsible for

Like a troupe of Chinese orphans
Trying to sell me fine wooden
Chess sets
Grotesque
Figurines which dance
To warped
Roughly hewn minuets
But the steps are fleeting

Days I'm dreaming
Of a juvenile courthouse in San Diego
Where I've missed a date
I fizzle and worry in my grandfather's felt
hat
About how much time
They are going to give me
Now that I'm 52

There are days I find
My way past
That battered bloody door

Days I'm accountable for

I go back in time

To convince the wrens
The robins refined
Bring me sugar all the time.

There's a cat flying off a bridge
Where that cold little boy lives.

There's a tarnished gun not very well hid
In the shaking hands
Of that strange little boy who never forgives

There's an acid rain that falls sideways

Where stolen food stamps and cigarettes are
Left burning in the light of
Keeping things that happen in this house
Always in this house
Shut your mouth, kid.

There are mornings
I sit in the cold of those evasive words
Knurled stomach knotting
Knowing in the back of my mind
No one is coming to save me
Nothing can stop the sky from falling.

So
I board the bus
To your funeral

With a soft
Kiss on my forehead
Your last breath on my eyes

These are the days I'm responsible for,

Days that never die.

The Razor of Your Smile

Shaving you
Father
The furthest thing
From my mind
Is you dying
For your skin
Is so soft
Warm and supple
Suffused with life
Your head
Touts fine soft hairs
As I turn you side to side
To reach the nooks
In the folds of your neck
Where wily whiskers bask
Defying my extra gentle strokes
My slightly trembling hands

I've never shaved anyone
But myself before

Is this what it means to let go
To be your eyes and ears
To give you my hands
Steady now
Warm the water just right
Choose a new razor
Make sure to wipe the excess clean

Shaving commercials
Of the 70s convinced us
A huge dollop of chemical
Laden goo was the answer
To all our problems as men
But I gently laud your face
With just the right amount
As I feel you smile underneath

Knowing I will never cut you

I touch you
Strange I've never touched
Your face before as an adult
It's just not a thing
We Black men do
I ask if you want me to shave
With or against the grain
You look baffled and say

Up

Always up

Guess I've been shaving wrong
All my life

Rinse away the white residue
Freshen up with brisk water
Pouring the suds away
I wish I could

Count the hairs in the stubble
I wish I didn't have to
Wash them away
Daydreaming I'll
Put them in a locket
Wear them like a shield

By the time I conceive
This fancy
They are gone
Carried away on gravity tethers
To their own special spot
Anonymous
Down in the Mississippi River

Have you ever had to shave
Your father
Shave him
Before you let him go?

Let's go one last time
To the casino, son

Let my smile be your razor
Let the soothing waters flow.

Famine

What does death eat?
It eats images
Gorges on poems
Death eats the breath
Of wandering golems
A wayward
Fallen angel
Who grows fat
At the behest
Of the banquets
Left by faceless
Senseless
Drones

Death eats the cruelty
That consumes the downtrodden
Who burp out flagrant
Condemnation
Of anyone who does not
Look
Feel
Act
Pray
Sing
Like them.

How does death groom?

Death raises a razor

At my neck when
I genuflect for self
Respect in the corner
Of a dark booth
Where fingers pry holes
In walls
Begging for my essence
To spit
On the floor.

Where does death loom?

Death floats in a mist
Blankets insincerity
With a noncommittal kiss
Can you live with this
It lisps
As it vomits chlorine
All over your bliss

How does death bloom?

Death sits on the shoulders
Of madmen with
Fingers on the button
While brown babies
In Gaza are vaporized
Into vengeance's oblivion

Death
Tears down the hands

That would feed them
Feed them
Feed them
Feed…

What does death eat?

It eats the apple of your eye
The crack of your ribs
The tearing of your ACL
The beam that tells the aliens we forgot how to cry
It eats your granny's stories
When she forgets the names
And her eyes start to focus
On strange men in bushes
Naked priests in the trees

Death eats your beliefs

But can't stand the taste
Of faith

Where does death wait?

In the center
Of your best intentions

Scraping your skull
Like a plate.

Imposter

The imposter
I convince myself I am
Looks longingly at
All these beautiful souls
Who get to dance with wolves
They stare right through me
With my hand me down
Lucidity.

A song in my head on repeat
Screams
Maybe one day
I'll be free
This impossible drone
Will eventually leave.

Could it be I'm
Too fat and toxic
Too old and traumatized
Too nervous, alone
Terrified
I'll never be enough
To calmly atone
For this terminal
Kaleidoscope of
Imposter syndrome.

The gentle voices between sleep
Whisper feverishly to me

That one day
I'll be good and strong enough
To finally believe
I no longer have to be outraged
My heart's on my sleeve

Though my belly rumbles
I no longer have to feed
Irrational beliefs.

I'm sitting alone in a prison
Writing love letters to Manson
From the Unabomber
Who hoards peanut butter
To bribe the guards.
I'm counting the hairs
On the head of a moth
Who tells me I have
Lost my soul.

Then
I remember
Moths don't talk.

23 Psalms 5 - Church and State

I'm on a train to nowhere
The sandwich cart is run by a dog
Who bites my face every time
I profess an adoration of God
I try to tell him God is not
A business venture
God is not the gavel in
McCarthy's hand
God is not whispering
Storm the Capitol
Shun your sons in dresses
Hate your daughters in tails
God is not a glass onion that
Revels in mystery illusion and pomp
God is not a prison tattoo
A prayer mat with a holster
A falling star with aim
A black body shot down
In the moonlight
Shining blue
In the rain

The dog bites my face again

Asks if I want mustard on my
Filet mignon

I tell him

I'm vegan

He doesn't want to talk
About
What
God
Is

Not

Anymore.

23 Psalms 6 - Black Male American

Statistically speaking
You and I aren't even supposed
To be speaking right now
Much less dreaming of
Nonstop smooth as butter
Conversations we've had
On 9 hour drives to the desert
To the mile-high mountains
To the bayous where the hounds
Ghost bark at us out of the shackles
But laugh as our people bind
Themselves to slave labor
Shoes made in Asian factories.

Statistically speaking
The ongoing Eugenics experiment
Of the Projects
The crack pipe
The needle full
The bubble
Should have taken us out by now
They tried Juvie
Work camp
Prison yard
Mandatory workout
Black Guerilla Family
Versus Jamba and Kumi infamy
They stabbed me in my sleep
They paired you with shells

Of people over whom even
Demons weep
There you were staring straight
Into Hell
On Sixth and Roosevelt
In a cheap motel
Where the radioactive roaches
Get high on crumbs
Get wasted on Malathion
You, you weren't meant to make it
Gambling Hustler Son
Of Mary born in the East La Slums

But here we are

Statistically speaking
My 'father' by now
Might have been a surrogate
Bank robber regaling me with
Tales of cheating and pimping
Trading me ramen for poems
As we rot away in a cell

Statistically speaking
My emotions should be stultified
Reduced down to a feeble thimble
Of shunned responsibilities
Dysfunctional kingdoms
Where scattered seeds plea for
Sunlight, their hair braided tight
Where the safety stops

When the social worker leaves.

But here we are
Making liars of them
Telling the naysayers
There's no quarter here
For that societal malaise
At all

Here we are
The most beautiful man
I've ever known
Being told by his son
I love you dearly
Every single day

Statistics

Were

Wrong.

This is my truth
This is my song

Black Male in America
This is where I'll stay.

23 Psalms 9 – Catgut Jazz

He explains time
Not like the way my drumsticks bounce
But in a way that breaks
Like an ill conceived
Hollandaise sauce
That just sort of floats
Around like a disembodied
Feral cat which refuses
The morsels of reality
We set out in a fancy
Dish labeled
Normalcy

I hold his hand
I listen to him breathe
Staccato
The way a storm hints
Arrival
Pensive
Like a burglar walking
Past lasers
I hold his hand
The way I hold on to my drumsticks
Keeping time
In a universe far away
Where there is no Facebook
There are no fancy metaphors
There is only the strange peace
A river must feel when

It breaks its shores

I stare like a hundred miles
Of railways going farther than
My eyes can see
I stare like a cloudburst
Waiting to meet the ground
I hold on like a Max Roach
Brush stroke to paint
The wall that separates us
With the great mystery words
Won't whisper
Where time evades
Where every breath is a gift
A windfall
A legacy
Of this just might be
His last night
His last breath

Knowing this

I'm just going to sit here
And watch that strange
Loping cat

Negotiate the fence.

Grief

DENIAL.

Wild rabbits ate my heart
There's a part of me
Still believes he's not gone
Wild rabbits trounced me
At checking my email
Embarrassing me on
Berkeley street corners
Dingy grey infused
With screaming cannabis
Wafting from the tables
Where provisional hippies
Sell silver to university students whose eyes
And wallets turn
Tepid at the sight of Deadhead symbols.

ANGER.

The wild rabbits ate the aux cable
They don't like Legendary
Pink Dots or the way Monty
Python songs will stop
An addict mid pull of fentanyl
From dumpster dived foil

The wild rabbits relish how the addicted recoil
The wild rabbits love to

Hear human blood boil
After all of
Those mascara experiments
On their vivisected siblings
Not so bold
The Wild rabbits they live in my soul
Where there's still a part of me
Convinced he'll walk through
My door

With his staccato pace
Just a little less tall
Bent with age
With a shock of white wisdom
Whiskers
Wielded on his handsome face

BARGAINING.

Wild rabbits
Thump on my pillow each morning
Calculate the Pennies baby
Don't be late
Iron out the wrinkles
Wild rabbits never tell me
When my fly is down
Wild rabbits
Sweep the homeless
From our wholesome towns
Wild rabbits
Become preachers instead

Of sponsors
Talk the newcomers
Into fear-based Christendom

DEPRESSION.

It's dangerous here, dear
I'd keep my eyes down

I'm waiting for the wild rabbits
To finally sleep
To calmly succumb
To slip past my nerves
Like gelatinous melatonin
Until the song that lives in their bared teeth haunts
My jugular no more
I'm waiting for the wild rabbits to snore
Until they forget the taste
Of a heart too stunned
To be warm.

Sleep sweet drowsy
Succulent conejos

Sleep my slippery
Sinewed rodents

Close those pink and brown eyes

Breathe
My chest indents

Breathe
Exhaling
Breathe
My chest insists

This isn't working.

ACCEPTANCE.

I still believe any second he'll come walking through that door…

To My Son

1. Prunedale

Dark words of sentimental
English boys
fertilized Christmas
Tree farms littered with
The feral teenage clumsiness
Of first forever never ever
Gonna die love
The grass is so fucking green love
The whole world is a cartoon
Except for us love
That I'm going to sneak out of my group
home to meet you in an artichoke field
Just to kiss you on the mouth
One more time
Kind of love
Dangerous
Break probation kind of
I'm shaking as you board the bus back to
Lake County love

You were conceived
In a rollicking cauldron
Of late nights fumbling over words we
barely knew
The meanings of
Left on wrinkly fill in every space of the
paper kind of love

Fecund
Nitrogen rich
Seaside soil
Soul love

Places between
Monterey Peninsula
Farm towns
Where no one
But hobos actually live kind of love

2. Castroville

One morning
I'd spent my last dime on a
Cheap too bright
Castroville hotel room

Against the group home rules
I was allowed to visit your mother

To see her back to the Salinas bus station
Where a ticket to Kelseyville
Purchased by Henry, my group home father,
awaited.

We lay in a bed
Covered in Cure songs
And she cried and cried and cried some
more

While that worn out tape played our favorite songs
Over and over on auto reverse
Nothing we could do but pack her bags and meet Henry at the door. He drove us to Greyhound where I had to all but drag her to the counter and onto the bus.

You were born of

I'm going to do everything in my power to be on the next bus

Because I'm crazy
Because surely, I will die
Without her
Because there was something in her teardrops
That morning that told me
We were no longer alone
In our shatterproof little world
Kind of love

Of this kind of poetry
you were born

Breathe

You,
You're invoking flowers
In the morn
Bright
Reflective
Petulant no more

You,
You're
Songs I've forgotten
Written into centuries
Our
Sinews strain to lift
Oppression
To
Beautiful struggle
Uncluttered lessons

You,
You're hot holy war
Where the infidelity
Of my hidden vulnerability
Is joyously absorbed.

You,
You're time I've spent
On an ancient moon
Watching the colonists
Get eaten alive

By the burning oxygen
Of their unkempt ambitions

I knew my tears
Wouldn't help when

You blew smoke rings
Life savers
You knew
Would never reach them.

Promises

I didn't want to write a poem
I've written too many poems
Every time I lose someone
Here come the words
Gushing out of the crust of stoicism
Like an anarchic geyser that heeds
No one, conceding to nothing
An autonomous phenomenon of
Meme phonemes and sibilant silken
Shudderings that don't quite
Embody the person I'm attempting
To memorialize
Immortalize even
Within the stodgy European
Trope of Shakespearean rambling

I said I wasn't going to write a poem
Because you
You are more than mere words
You are the tears of joy
In the songs of birds
Who stare blankly at me crying
In the rain
My mumbling unheard
Not even interested in knowing
My name
They don't really care who I am
They keep singing

I said I wasn't going to beseech
The butterflies or bees to carry
My prayers to you
I wasn't going to try to tell
The winds to soothe
The river to coo
The moon to unburden
Itself in a blanket of clouds
Talk to me of you
In another space
Another time
Possibly standing right
In front of me
In a dimension I'm not
Privy to seeing

I promised I wouldn't write
About how I can hear you
Clear as day
Two days after you left
People might think I'm crazy
People might think
I lost all respect
For Judeo-Christian traditions
The dead die
You mourn
You bury them
You don't hear them
You don't talk to them

But I'm not listening

I'm trying not to write this poem

I'm failing miserably
Obviously
Because your voice
Was my favorite song
The first I learned of rhythm
The painting of emotion
Before I had language
Before I became
Erudite or eloquent
Before I knew the meaning of poem
Your voice carries on…

I will not write this
I will not write this

No, I will scream this
Until the birds
The butterflies
The bees
The river
The mountains
The sky
The moon
The flowers
The babies not yet born
The ancestors you greet

Know
You are more than mere words

You

Are

Poetic song

You

Are

Sacred

Psalms to me.

Section Three

The House Where Tornadoes Lived

Trauma

I remember your
Crooked little smile
Eyes closed tightly
Poised atop a wobbly washing machine
With your hair on fire
Cigarette angled perfectly
Nonchalant
Daring the whole world
To ask just who the hell you thought you
might be

I remember how you loved to fight
Riding your bicycle blind into
Ocean View Avenue's traffic
Every night
All the drunks watched
Passive
Placing bets on who'd steal your wallet

You were a
Clockwork subterfuge
Time bomb with your skin dyed
Pink and blond

Tethered to a vivisected ballerina's
Quackery clever
Clinging to dramas pondered by
Little tragic men lost in the rain
Whose handsome winsome faces

Melt off from the pain of
Dancing on tsunamis
With a plastic static haze

We saw you flickering
Back and forth in blighted delight
Like the heartbeat of that elevator operator
Who caused the Tulsa riots
We all knew you were lying

Then
Trauma grinds its teeth
Puts on a vague stare
Curses everyone
Everywhere

When
You so willingly
Confused acrimony with chivalry
Serenity with doubt
Codependency with serenity
Articulation with clout
Drooling
Shaking maniacally
With an axe in your hands
Waiting
For the world to just
STOP!!!

Bloody Mary

It's horrendous down this dark hall
The one you know
Bloody Mary haunts
Which ends in a glow in the dark
Poster of a green skinned alien waving

We don't know if it's hello or goodbye
Or fuck you, you human piece of garbage
Because we can't speak alien
At 3 in the morning
When he comes into my room
All too human and I drown in silence
So much silence as the monsters
Light cigarettes and eat salted plums
In the doorways, his drunken breath
Berates me, turns me over and over
Deflates me until like a breached beach ball
I sit there in my own piss

The hallway laughs with a hiss.
I miss my mother
As he walks away laughing.

Bloody Mary haunts this hall
The one I can never walk
That one creaking board always snitches me
out.
I can never
Sleep

I weep
I set the neighborhood houses on fire

No one listens

Bloody Mary lights another one
With the very same lighter I stole
To strike the blazes

28 days later
He's back in my room
At 3 am turning me over and over
Like a shovel full of dead concrete
Sprinkled with lime and tossed in a corner
To cry myself hoarse and scream into
My pillow until I'm numb

The aliens and Jason Vorhese
All sit in front of a scrambled signal from
The Playboy channel eating hog maws
From the skull of a boy they ignore
As they squint and draw closer to the screen
To try and make out a glimpse of a boob.

Bloody Mary floats through
With her good Indian Hair
She doesn't really care

As I watch him walk away laughing again
I miss my mom
I steal all the house guns

It's the silence of death
That overtakes the night
I cannot move
Paralyzed by his weight

The smell of cheap cigarettes
The bed is wet
Is it blood or piss
Tears or cum?

I can't tell anymore
I cannot tell anyone
I miss my mom

As Bloody Mary pokes the alien
And sings to it an interspecies love song

The hallway yawns voraciously

As he laughs
Walking away in the dark
Chanting

Bloody Mary
Bloody Mary
Bloody Mary
Bloody Mary
Bloody Mary
Bloody Mary
Bloody Mary
Bloody Mary

Richelle

Shootings
Rising death rates
Goon squads
Election's on the take
Right hate
Left hate
Brain aches
Another word from the President
Assuredly fake

But I just watch you

You're brown heaven
Scents of soft chocolate
Centuries dipped
Succulently
Kissed

The whole world is clamoring
Like Fred and Ester arguing.
The windshield is greasy
Weaving as we argue over who's driving.
News never soothing
Disinformation dividing
The death toll bell
Peals louder
Louder

Lives falling into a chicken shredder

But I just watch you

You're brown heaven
Scents of soft chocolate
Centuries dipped
Succulently
Kissed

Arrogancia

In the muddle of

The morning

Field trip

To the

Santa Cruz

Tide pools

A little boy

Leans in

Asks a crab

If fish ever imagine

They can walk

The crab latches

Tightly onto the boys

Hand

Says

We might

But we imagine the pain

Of your domain

So it stops

The little boy

Relishes bleeding

Though he keeps

Pretending

Thrashing

The crab never let go

In the muddle of

The morning

Field trip

To the

Santa Cruz

Tide pools

Rabies

I want to cast a spell
Subliminally
That tells you to hug
The man with no hands
Piloting the helicopter
In the folds of your brain
Demanding you
Turret fire dopamine
Into the dense burning forests
Of shame
Where the laughter of lost children
Mothered by good intentions
Goes dancing in invisible flames

I wanted to rebuke the devil
But I forgot his Instagram handle
I wanted to join your posse
In search of you
But I'm stuck on a legless horse
Who's terrified of becoming glue

There's a storm coming in.

There's a party happening
In my mind but no one's talking
There's a place I've never been
Seems so familiar
There are lions stalking
On their bellies

There's a telekinesis laden rat
Who sells discount heart attacks
There's a slovenly wolf that tells me

There is no cure for rabies
There are no assured maybes
There is no revolution on Hulu baby
There is no one in the pilot's seat

Can you hear me?

Restraint

I did not call all weekend
I did not write you poems
I stayed in my little bed
I was a good boy
Will you throw me a bone?

I did not once view your
Facebook profile
I didn't mention you to my barber
My sponsor only knows you as Berkeley
All my poet friends think you're
Likely imaginary

Will you please pet me?

I wiggled my butt in the mirror
Was it pert enough
Is my chest to become your pillow
Shaped just right to fit
Your pirate locks
In the throbbing center
That goes soft
When you choose me as your dock

I slept all weekend
On your porch
I did not talk to the neighbors
I did not pry the lock

I played patty cake with your cat
Who, like me, was once feral
I practiced my best smile
She did not scratch it off.

I sat in the feeling of daring you to kiss
Not once wondering if you'd thought of me

While the band played on
I sat here watching my tongue
Wishing you'd just throw that damn ball
Just once.

Lost

Lisa wanted to know
Where the wolves go
When they're happy
When the saliva
Drips off their incisors
For joy
Not because they are
Rattled by the acid
That being hungry
Bleeds into their beautiful
Forms
Making their faces
Lips recoiled
Masks of alarmed harm

She wanted to know
Where the wolves go dance
When they let down their
Defenses
Lick each other's ears
Touch noses
Exchange whelping stories
Share holes in fences
Where water can be found
Stare at the moon
In lucid profundity
Until the backs of
Their eyes fill with
So many tears

They have to cheer
To clear their throats
Until mother Luna retreats

Lisa wanted to know
Who sees the wolves
When they're not angry
Who reassures them
The night
The hunt
The unease
Will eventually leave
Who Lullabies
Them to serenity
Who settles their hackles
When winter's spindly comb
Demands disarray

Who nullifies their
Senses catapulted
Like kicks of rabbits
In their preying gaping maws

Lisa wonders if the wolves
Know

Love is the law
Love under will

As she roams the forest
Lost three days now

Highly aware of the pack's
Footfall
Closing in.

Black
By Embers the Cat

They have me on camera
Everywhere.

Rolled blanket burritos

Nice comfy clean smelling human burritos

Who squeak when I run across their backs
Play dive bomb from the windows.
They tell me I am pregnant with joy
How they long to have grandchildren

I merely gawk and demure
Place a hesitant paw over their lips
As if to reassure

Cameras
Everywhere

Don't let slip that stare!!!

Music Theory #2 - The Minor Chord

We've been practicing
This
    Syncopated
One
    Two

Pause

    One

Pause

    One

        Two

Walk into the chapel all week

Dress rehearsal
        After school
Practicing
        In my sleep
Practicing
        When no one
        Is watching at PE

It's Easter morning
        We have that good
Spring Valley

                    Guest preacher
Whose light skinned daughter
                    Always likes to stare
At me when I pass the plate
                    For offering

I'm seriously crushing
                    This is the morning
Everything has to be just right
                    She has these fiercely
Bright
                    But quiet green eyes
Under the shade
                    Of perfectly coiled bangs
She's a little cross eyed
                    But, I like that sort of thing

I've been practicing
                    Shining my shoes twice
Pretending to tie my tie
                    Imagining I'll step up to her
At the barbecue after the service
                    Offer her some trivia about
Collard greens, chicken wings
                    See her giggle move her bangs

I've been practicing

        One
Two
        Pause

   Step
            One
Two

         Pause
Step

I've got my purple and mauve
Mount Zion Baptist church
Junior choir robe on
Over my Montgomery Wards
Extra itchy polyester excuse for
A suit for young men

I'm behind the home preacher's son

Soon and very soon

Clap
              We are going to see the king

One step

           Clap
Two

Pause

Clap

Soon and very soon

Clap

      One

Two

   Clap
We are going to see the king

Hallelujah

Pause

Clap

And just as I see her honey-colored skin
Just as I imagine her eyes are on me
Just as I think she sees me smiling
Not with my mouth
But my whole being

I trip on the hem of my choir robe
And go down like
Her father says a man will
When he's drowning in sin
I go down like one more sack
Of cotton that weights barely
Nothing but carries enough gravity
To crash Venus into Mercury
If the sun were not looking
I crash down like the Space shuttle

Right on my goofy face
Right in front of the whole church

Bringing down the home preacher's
Son and everyone in front of him

A scuffle ensues

Now the rhythm is gone

Two
Two.   One?

Clap?

Soon and clap very step soon pause
Clap again
Shit

I say shit at the top of my lungs
On Easter morning
Right in the middle of the
Junior choir walk in
As the guest preacher's daughter
Starts laughing loud enough
To rouse the sleeping deacons

The organ player hit a chord
So pragmatically sour
So perfectly out of place

So longing
Begging
For the congregation's
Attention
While the laughter was building

That chord said look
Look at me
I'm poor and starving
I'm missing teeth or shoes
Barely surviving
But beatific all the same
Strangely familiar
Yet not quite matching
One foot shorter than the other

Dancing on the 1 and 3
Like a model with one eyebrow
Shaven

It was in that moment

Struggling to compose myself
Picking up the home preacher's
Pissed off son
Being glared at by my foster father

Having hurled an expletive
Being the bad foster son

It was at that moment

My music education began

Though I did not know it yet
I had just learned

The very essence of the minor chord.

Collapse

It doesn't hurt like that

I just forget to breathe
When you want to feel my heart
Simply stand next to a dying star.

If you
Hold your breath
You'll forget the sparks
All the bountiful colors
That fade into a canopy
Of jeans crafted from larceny
On sale
In the church of stunning mediocrity

Stolen valor flavors
Mint Juleps with stubborn airs
Listless portents uttered
By anhedonic eyeless witches
Stirring a caldron
Named regret
Daring you to stare

I stood on the corners
Where serial killers picked their teeth
With the bones of infants who'd no longer
weep.
I watched them gesture to one another
To wipe the brain matter off their cleats,

I never thought of them as athletes
But oh my, does it take a lot of energy
To crush a human being

If you want to feel my heart
Make your way past
The high school where troubled teens
Steal Pink Floyd lyrics
To teach themselves to be poets.
Creep carefully past the grocery stores
Where shoplifted cartons of cigarettes
Give the same kids that William Burroughs growl
In their burgeoning voices as they are apprehended
Two steps outside the door by dour security guards.

It doesn't hurt like that anymore
But oh, my are my lungs ever sore
From yelling into this
Ceaselessly bored collapsed star

Duality/Dystopia

Inside of you there are two wolves
Why do you have wolves inside of you
Is there something wrong with you
Maybe it's just that you're crazy…

Inside of you there are two wolves
One has rabies, the other is convinced he's a squirrel

One is not taking their medication
The other has been apprehended selling drugs to rabbits

One has been lobotomized
The other is avoiding child support

One owns a fully automatic assault rifle
The other just loves to knit gloves for protesters

One just told me they're vegan
While the other one feigns gluten intolerance.

Inside of you there are two wolves…
And again, why do you have wolves inside of you
I mean, I'm not trying to kink shame you
But maybe it's just that you're crazy

Inside of you there are two wolves
One believes in voter suppression
The other one won't even bother registering

One just stole my car
While the other offered me a foot massage

One is bipolar
The other has depressive tirades

One loves chocolate
The other sings off key at goth weddings

One has complex PTSD
And attacks the other who practices Reiki

One has bulimia
While the other wastes away stoically

Inside of you there are two wolves

Which one do you feed?

Trauma 3 - The Ghost

I woke up at 3:32 am tonight to stumble to my restroom. Passing the open door of my room, I notice the hood light above my stove is on and standing there staring at me was a haggard little boy. His eyes burn away my stupor which swiftly escalates to utter shock as my need to pee disappears like any sense of responsibility the rioters from January 6 might have felt. The little boy stares at me from under his eyes with a maniacal sort of silence where his teeth are somewhat bared and a trace of madness glints from his eyes. He starts to walk towards me down the hallway he struts slowly like syrup, slowly like trauma. I turned to see my wife snoring and my little dog curled up beside her. Then much to my consternation I see my own sleeping body, hand clutching the remote as I lay there on my back, asleep.
The lump in my throat grows larger, my heart pounds and I realize the absurdity of it all. Does my astral body really have a heartbeat? By this time the child is in front of me. His hair is a reddish auburn burly mess of unkempt naps. He wears only a pair of pastel pink cutoff shorts, nothing more, barefoot and bare chested... I shiver as I notice my body turn over to face my wife, startling the puppy who does not notice me

there in the door being accosted by the apparition in my hallway.
The child slowly raises a hand in which he holds a snub nosed .38 pistol. His hand shakes ever so slightly as he points the gun at me then lets it fall slackly to his side. He shakes his head, running the thin fingers of his other hand through his hair. He gnashes his teeth and thrusts the gun at me again. This time choking through the tears.

"Why didn't you shoot him, why did you let him keep hurting me? You had the guns, you slept right next to his room. You could have taken this gun here and just ended it. No more abuse from him. No way he could have hurt anyone else after that. You should have just shot him in his sleep one night."

Suddenly I recognized this child. Horrified, I am face to face with my trauma embodied in an apparition roving my hallway at 3:30 a.m. while my wife snores and I grumble in my sleep.
I stumble slightly backward, wanting to slip back into my body, be at rest, not confronted by this angry young child in his pink shorts pointing a gun at me and crying his eyes out.

I conjure a bit of calm and start to think of what to say at this moment.

The gun is raised again as the child goes on to say, "Since I couldn't hurt him, I hurt you, I hurt everyone you ever loved, everything you ever created, every single word you wrote, every time someone loved you, I was there with this gun wondering if anyone could see me. There were those who were psychic, who sensed me as some sort of magical being. There were those who could see me whispering in your ear. There were those who wanted to reap this anger they sensed, mistaking it as dominance, hungering to be eviscerated. There were witches and there were others carrying their own wounded children. We fought, we hid, we touched curiously and fled as soon as we knew..."

The gun is the gun of my Foster father which I used to steal when I was a child, that child in my hallway now. I always wondered why I stole guns all the time. Now I know. There was a part of me that wanted to shoot my abuser, the man who stole my sleep and took my innocence. That child never went away. That child followed me my whole life, unseen...

"I know you. I knew you all along. Lurking in the shadows of every regret I ever had. Every heart I ever lured and broke. I know you and I had a feeling you'd show up one day again. Maybe not like this, but sure again and again and again...until you understand

I forgave them
All of them
For hurting you
For putting the gun in your hand.
For letting you run around barefoot
Half-naked
Wounded
Afraid

I forgave them and I was no longer afraid

Of you

Of what you had done
Or what you could do

Because by forgiving them

I loved you."

The child stared longingly at me
Hoping one sliver of resentment might blossom. Just one moment of hatred might rise so he could point the gun at my head and shoot me down.

I turn to walk to my body. The child laughs.
I peek over my shoulder as he fades.
My alarm is going off. It's 6 a.m. Time to work.
Time to help others confront the child roaming their hallways trying to shoot down their spirit.
Their very own custom-made trauma.

Section Four

Love it Political

Say Their Names

Stonewall was a riot
Started by a black trans woman
Marsha P Johnson
Say her name
The March on Washington
Was organized by a Black Queer man
Bayard Rustin
Say his name
A man
Who quietly stood in the shadows
Of a movement
That would maybe let him
Lead the choir but still not
Allow him to
Show his face at reunions
If he asked to bring his husband along.

I once lived
In a quaint apartment with the founder
Of the Sisters of Perpetual Indulgence
Who explained over and over
How her father
Who was alcoholic
Would beat her
To within an inch of
Her life every single time
He couldn't force her to be
Exactly who she was not

Out of this
Sister Vicious was born
Fleeing Iowa
To start a band of merry gay nuns
Helping the downtrodden

I listened with ire
Wide eyed
Saw the clouds of thick
Smoke being blown in the air
Realizing that at a certain point the trauma
Overtook the movement
We were studying hanky
Codes and flags, but no one could hear
What Sister Vicious was saying:

It hurts not belonging
It hurts bleeding
It hurts pleading
To simply be seen

What's her name
Say her name
Marsha P Johnson
What's her name
Say her name
Sister Vicious Power Hungry Bitch!!

Rainbow icee swirls
Bud Light Pride booths

All the colors in the world
Can't change the fact

Stonewall was a riot

Guuuuuuurl!!!

This is the history I learned
Sitting at that table with Sister Vicious
Smoking
Witnessing the exhalation
Of a movement
Understanding
That trauma loves
Forgetting

Stonewall

Was

A

Riot

Started

By

A

Black

Trans

Woman.

What's her name
Say her Name

Marsha P Johnson!!!

What's her name
Say her name

Sister Vicious Power Hungry Bitch!!!

Bertha

I met Bertha at a bar
Bertha had a cat
Named Pickles
Who could talk

Pickles had caught Jesus
Stealing Bertha's car
Pickles said Jesus had gone woke
Pickles resented the fact that Jesus
Was nodded off on Skid Row.

Bertha loved those trucks
Flying Trump 2024 flags
Driven by Russian rifle bearing patriots

Pickles had told her
To attend the insurrection
Pickles feared miscegenation
Pickles hated reproductive protections
Pickles was absolutely terrified the birth dearth
Would mean the end of Caucasians.

Intrigued,
I got another whiskey
For this disheveled
Looking woman.

Bertha said

I'm not racist
I love Clarence Thomas
She told me
Pickles had a secret crush on
Candace Owens.

Bertha tried to convince me
Of some grand LGBTQ conspiracy
That drag queens were out to get me
They were mutilating babies
In basements, after all
She and Pickles had heard it on Hannity.
Every night together they'd watch Fox news
Pickles was sick of filthy immigrants
Pickles despised lazy communists
Collecting welfare checks
Pickles loved student debt
Because it kept wage slavery intact
Pickles only smoked American cigarettes
Pickles had collected lots of PPE loans
To stock up on catnip
Because, after all
Pickles deserved it!

Bertha leaned in
The cheap liquor
On her breath
She said you're different
You listen
You don't talk like
Them

You don't act like
Them
You're kinda cute
What's your name?

In my head, I said

My name is gay rights
My name is cities in flames
My name is hands off our bodies
My name is gender affirming care
My name is mental health equity
My name is black lives matter
My name is George Floyd
My name is land back
My name is too late, Bertha
The drag queens already got me.

But from my mouth
Came simply, politely
Anthony.

Later that night my phone dinged
It was a Facebook request from
The woman whose cat
I was quite sure
Hacked voting machines

Bertha Van Ation wants to be your friend.

I think I should really quit drinking.

Babylon Chant

Everything is personal
Everything is political

Prince writhing on the stage
In his girlfriend's high heels
With her stockings acting
Merely as a banana peel
Made all the more slippery
By the thrumming drums
Gut punching Bass
Illustrating perfect possession
In his wild waistline which
Rose and fell without permission
Like that smile upon
His childlike face

To one day be erased
By a synthetic opiate
They now mix up in the truck stop
Bathroom sinks with recipes
Downloaded from Tor
In disappearing ink.

Everything is personal
Everything is political

Nancy Reagan could never
Just say no
To the fame promised

In Hollywood backrooms
If she would
Just simply blow.

Hidden in the White House bathroom
She sneaks a puff of a Lucky Strike
Covers the scent with Ozium
Thinking about how she never became
Marilyn, but she got the best man
Who lets her deprive
The gays of medicine
Watch them shrivel like
The non-filtered in her hand
Practicing her best smile
Prepares to pretend satisfaction
In front of the whole nation
Denying her ongoing oral fixation

Because
Everything is personal
Everything is political

Crack cocaine in a war-torn ghetto
Burns not nearly as smooth
As the Contra propaganda
Not smooth as a thalidomide baby's brain
Not smooth as the hips of HIV positive
dancers
On Soul Train
Not smooth like the once unmarred lungs of
the Marlboro Man

Sweet cocaine pops and blisters like
smuggled guns
In the hands of the traumatized
grandchildren of hooked veterans
There's a War on Drugs
But the drugs won

Thank You, Mr. Reagan
For the trickle down

Everything is personal
Everything is political

"Come we go chant down Babylon more time."
Bob Marley

Breakfast in Bed

Crooked smile
Wakes me
Sacral
Makes me howl

Husky
Hybrid
Cute enough
Gets away
Every time
This hand
Licked
Not bit
Pantomimes
Bliss

Holy mother
Dew drop pearl
Lips

By now
You have

Slightly
Sneered
Near the helix
Of these nets
Trying
To catch your fix

Do you always
Serve
Breakfast
In bed

I'll walk
Tenderloins
Barefoot
Backwards
With curling toes

To plant on your moon
A single decorative
Suffocating rose.

Labyrinth

Doctor, wake up
The ink spots
In my brain
Are flirting with forms
Of electroshock
That spiral into
Chaotic unlicensed
Rorschach stains

Doctor, wake up
A lazy river tells me to
Tickle her innards
When I choose to chase ambitious
Rabbits to death
Trying to interpret vague laughter.

Doctor, wake up
My car won't stop beeping
I can't stop driving
An app invites me
To meet death
In a desperation flavored
Room where the handcuffs are brittle
Where the demons hand me brooms
To sweep the tears of Eros
From outside activism's tomb.

I dreamt you were a giraffe

Who could reach the tail feathers of
Pterodactyls
In a Time Machine run on
Broken principles
Precarious gaffes
Of polyphonous particles that stones circles
Can never wrap.
Salt sculptures in the
Playa dust where
Sepulchers in the church aisles are burning
sulfur for
Incense when the batted eyes of go-go
dancers
Create only shadows
Woven of wisp and chance.

Doctor, wake up
The Minotaur wants to
Walk in the serious moonlight holding the
hand
Of Medusa's stillborn
Daughter.

Dear Doctor,
Will you respect me in the morning
Will you promise to call?
Will you run when I ask you
Is this included in my insurance costs?

Buzzards Bay

When we walk in the quiet forest
You're back in your body

When we crowd into your
Steamy small shower
I'm in your body

When the pain digs deep
Into your shoulder
Long fingers capped with
Nebulas

You leave your body

I stare at your aura

Your aura seems lonely

Not nearly as lovely

As when you
Call me to your body

Terrified
Of the forest
I could never be

Thee Psychick President

So, you say you're an empath?

What if you're just a very
Very hyper vigilant
Sociopath with no mingling
Skills whose isolation
Has convinced you that
You can see through walls
Walk backwards into mirrors
Interpreting the bird songs
Into garbled water cool
Gibberish that's never quite clear

You go Saturday Night Live
Dancing with howling spirits
Go chasing down hungry ghosts
In Rome
With destiny's spear
But still can't find deliverance

Maybe you think
You're just naturally
Gifted
You're magically autistic
You hear all the colors
Taste all the sounds
Talk to feral cats and dogs
Translating the dead language
Of rain before it hits the ground

You bring to every lean to
Hovel on skid row
A sacred angelic
Glow of
Tea tree scented
Tesseracts
Palatial palaces of palaver
In the ice caps' melting snow

But have you ever considered
My dear friend
You might
You could just be
A flaming narcissist?

What's that you say?
You're the psychic president?
Excuse me for blaspheming

I'm sure you find it demeaning
I think you're just babbling
Laughing all the way to the bank
To cash in that belief
Everyone's out to get you

Because, after all
You ARE
The most important
Person in the room.

Covid

It only takes a push
All the China dolls just fall apart
Just a tiny little touch
To make the whole world stop
Now melting like the film
Caught on a projector bulb
It only takes a little snake
To bring on the venom suds
Which bathe
In a curiously piquant flavor
The nefarious behavior
Of your crack smoking neighbor
Who spies on your children
Writes down everything you
Are or are not doing

All it took was a tiny plucky virus
To reveal what was lurking deep inside us.
Just a minuscule little nudge
To make humanity its own worst judge
Don't talk to strangers
They might fight or shoot you
Or even worse, cough on you
There's danger at the edge of town
Since this silence came careening down
All it took was a circus
To bring out all the slobbering
Gun toting clowns.

Porcelain is oh so precious until broached
By the gravity of truth
The floor's greedy touch
If it's getting all too much
Just call your congressman
Who doesn't give a fuck
Who
Stuck drinking in a bathtub
Sees condors circling this burning church.

All it takes is a flick of the switch
To turn heaven to a sand sandwich
We're dancing on the crumbling cliff

All that's required is a love hate relationship
With a ventilator's labored sighing

To send the arrows of your
China doll heart flying.

The Avenging Angel of Election Year

I forgot what it feels like
To not shrug
Sweep all emotions
Swiftly under a rug

I sit here in the swirling
Lights of Eden
The Angel behind me
Screams Ditto
Kiddo
As they swing a flaming
Sword
Persona non grata
Won't work anymore

They tell me I can't
Stand with my cardboard
Sign begging for candy
On the 15th street off-ramp anymore

They tell me the soft white underbelly of my illusion of a once great America has exploded.

They tell me the man in the red tie lies and cheats on his taxes and wants nothing more than outright scorched earth revenge. I believe them

I try to love my neighbor
But my neighbor always
Ignores the gift of desperation
I leave at her door

The Angel says
We don't know that miracle around these
parts anymore.

You have bullets or ballots
Church pews or liquor stores

Coping or conundrums
Children behind electric fences

Whisper in their native tongues
About the inevitability of war.

The National Anthem

I've said enough
What's your sign
Who's your daddy
What key fits your collar
How many senses does it take
To make you
Make me
Break a dollar?

Said too much
Now smoke a cig
Cover yourself with bacon grease
Launch into the polling place
With a flag tattooed over your face
Famous for exactly 13 minutes
Chewed up, savored then released
Back into the streets
Where you can buy a gun for a sack
Where you can open a sky wide
Hole in your head
With merely a hit of crack.

Said all I could
The auto censors zap us
Walking along with disheveled throngs
To get a compostable bowl of soup
From the church that offers vaccinations
Whose sidewalk is littered with failed
Trial victims all gasping for air

We step over them
Extremely careful what we think
Lest we should get lasered by the robots
Who patrol these streets

Oh no
I've said enough
What's your political party, baby
Flick your Bic?
Between Death and Slavery
Tell me, Honey Chile
Which would you savor?

Jose,

Can you see?

Jose,

Answer me!!!

Breathless

The way the world ends?

You're looking listlessly to the clouds
Praying a plastic obtuse
Bent song
To a horrified
Jesus who can't hear you
Too busy answering the prayers
Of Republicans
Wailing
Because His father has gone
Grey green purple blue
Gangrene in the peep show booth
Trying to heal his age-old wounds
With harlots and stale hot chocolate
That never soothes

He lights a crack pipe then presses it
Between your eyes
PSHHHHHHH
Leaving an angry red Bindi sizzling

There

Now you're enlightened.

I'll watch the world implode with you
Hypnotized by susurrus
Of distant Sidewinder missiles

Which lisp hallelujah
Sweet by and by
Serenaded by sweet
Psalm chanting aliens
Who snatch the Bible
From your
Febrile
Fleeting
Forsaken
Praying

Hands

Love is Revolutionary

I'm not going to hide
I will not be demure
I will wear the wrong shirt
To church
I will paint my nails
I will dance with heathens
I will not be polite
If you voted to suppress me
I will buy a gun
I will learn to shoot it
Pew pew, baby
Come and see.

I am not going to run
I will talk to my soulmates
In India
In Brazil
I will show off my beautiful
Partners
There's not a damn thing
You can do to make them
Less stunning
I'm going to kiss too long on the lips and get lost in a
Tongue that splits
A tongue that swirls around
My shattered expectations
Assures me
This is my world

This is my joy

You can't steal it

I'm going to make you happy
I mean we're gonna have to
Change these sheets.
I'm going to sneer as I cheer
On your liberation
I'm going to spin you in
A dark club where everyone
Scowls to smile
I will never ask your age
I will grow pudgy with your
Moaning growls.

Because we're all really just
Kids inside
I mean like baby goats
Butting heads
Eating out of garbage cans
Chasing raccoons
Being completely adorable
But screamingly unmanageable

I'm going to set you free
I'm not going to leave
I'm going to watch you heal
From the cheap thrill
Of acrimonious victory
I'm going to feed your beliefs

I'm going to be your
Liminal Thought Criminal

Until death no longer knocks
On your door

Until we stand on the streets watching the
Capitol
Burn down to the cinders
Of an idea we were never invited to explore

I will be there

Until the giant falls.

Short All-Purpose Love Poem

If you

Like it

I love it.

Section Five

A Speculative Future Past

Religion

I wanted to be a preacher, but I realized
early on I did not wish to sing praises
To a far-off entity who heard my cries in the
deep dark night
But was too busy laughing at bumbling
televangelists to help me

I didn't think such a god would be so dumb
as to ask me to be very quiet in the midst of
hell while granting me the sword of a fire
flecked silver tongue to lick nine-inch nails
before they met the flesh of his only
begotten son.

I didn't think such a god would be so
arrogant as to sip a diet soda while glibly
watching Reagan getting shot by Hinckley,
bullets passing through the skull of
Kennedy.

I asked myself time and time again what had
happened to that once great white man in the
sky who traded his progeny for a stolen
Bugatti, an ivory handled handgun to wave
around protesting Emmet Till's memorial in
a poverty-stricken hatred soaked alcoholic
little town in Mississippi.

I wanted to be a preacher. Orate, pontificate, gesticulate, even gyrate.
But I quickly became afraid the only god that would hire me was likely some murder prone deranged clown who lived underground chewing on the cover of a book human skin bound.

I wanted to be a preacher as a kid, lead hymns from the pulpit
Praise a power greater than my gaping worthlessness, collect tithes in a silver basket

Buy Janis Joplin that Benz.

But I couldn't sing on key

So, I just became a poet instead.

Famous (with an F flat)

You laid tarot cards out
The gypsy in you saw
Bad omens
I just saw a beautiful woman
Whose hair was always on fire
Because she thought
Being famous meant
You'd never expire

Guess I should have
Never given you
My torch lighter

The whole world's on fire

Famous with an F flat

You stared at my ashen bones
Wondering why
The extinguishers
Were password locked

I sang to the ghost
Of your dog

The dog was tone deaf

The dog's morals
Eclipsed

By the need for
Just one more salty snack

The dog never listens

You tell me
The cards always
Land on their backs

The whole world is on fire now
It sizzles

Famous
With an F flat.

Open Mic

Why do we show up
Why do we write
Why do we writhe before you
Tongues wagging
Fighting
The dying of the light

Why do we chase butterflies
With flaming knives
Why do we seduce Medusa
With wobbly glass eyes
Why do we stand here
Asking why

Is it for the glamour
The broken back massagers
The chance to look in your soul
Recognizing the gleaming
Sudden satisfaction of premonition

For it's not the words or the sound
But the soul of the silence
That skulks busking
Between the words

It's the hope that I'll see you again
Briefly if only to incrementally
Understand the sinew touched by
Dew which moves your hands

To hold a feather out
Tickling Atlas
Tempting the turtle upon
Whose back the world stands
To dance

Why do we do it
With nothing to prove
Why would I desire to move you
To tears
To jeers
To cheer
To draw near
To hear
The wheezing of a dying star
The absence of a recovered alcoholic
At the haunted indentation at the bar
The screeching fingernails
Of the professor turned bard
As he roadmaps
The course to freedom
On asbestos lined whiteboards
The faceless hedonism of Jim Morrison
Driving a car made of chicken bones
Fueled by the monotone musings
Of beat poets no one heard reverberate
Who sang to Black Panthers that stalked
Dignity a little too late.

Why do we do this
What is our fate

To collect the tears of muses
On our glowing iPhones
To starve the hounds of hell
Waiting for our demise to whet their plates

Why do we do it?

Because the birth of black holes
Simply can't wait.

Visceral Incorporated

Visceral Incorporated called me in a dream
The overzealous voice on the other end
Did not even wait for me to say hello
It just started spieling

It was one of those deep warm voices
That tells you medication side effects
In a way that somehow
Makes explosive diarrhea seem appealing

Here at Visceral incorporated
We have Mexican cartel video theatre
In bright 4K
24 hours a day
Where you can watch the third world
Lay out it's wards
In wholesome cuts and fillets

Where discount machetes
Come with multilingual instruction manuals
Declaring murder is cheap
But why be messy?
You don't want that
Infidel blood spoiling the new
Kayne West Jordan's on your feet
So, get yourself some emergency room
Booties, get yourself some
Disposable Gucci, buy a full
Length leather jacket that doubles

As a tourniquet once the Kevlar
Has been depleted
Get yourself some wholesale
Uranium enriched ammo
For your ghost printed AR15
Buy a genuine bloodstained hood
Of the Klan for a mere 15 dollars, ma'am.

Get yourself a whites only drinking fountain
To install upon the trail of the world's
Highest mountain. Watch the foster children
Exploited for free labor or cheap pleasure
Soaked in trauma told to recite speeches
insisting one day they'll be better
They'll be mayors
They'll be lawyers
While being shaped into fodder
For rich kid laughter
Look at that caveman go
Look at him dodder
Look at him kiss my poor
Poetry-seduced daughter.

You can watch power mad African lords
Roast their enemies
Over surplus
Black market
Napalm campfires
High on Khat
Or whatever they're calling
The thing that makes black men go

Whack this week
Staring off into manifestos
Posted by Russian trolls
Instructing them
To burn it all down

We have Stepford wives
Dating killer clowns
We have a contest going
To see who can make the most
Schoolchildren lay down
We have a thriving market on
Proclaiming the Vice President a Ho
Waving tiki torches
Chanting whatever the Kremlin told them

I think I took too much melatonin
But, I can never manage to hang up on them.

A Little To The Left

It's 2050
The manufacturers of
Beyond Meth
Have entered into
A horrid conflagration
With the producers
Of Fauxtenyl,
(The newest
Synthetic opioid
Being marketed as an over
The counter 'sleep' aid)
As to which one of their products
Should be shipped to the
Multibillion dollar
Moon prison colony
Where all the inmates
Work around the clock
Producing gene splice roasts
3D printing
Sequenced pork butts
Making robot chickens
Who lay eggs that dance
The Electric Boogaloo
When you cook 'em.

Their corporate robots fight
Around the clock on select streaming
services

To see which drug will be leaked into the
oxygen system.
Meanwhile,
On Earth
The President is hooked
On bathtub melatonin
Laced with Fauxtenyl
She's
Been seen watching
Soft White Underbelly interviews
On repeat
In her underwear while being
Serviced by parolees who
Want to 'work' off their
Indiscretions
Somewhere other than the damp dark moon
colony

Their swift soft fingers weaving
Hyperspeed Dopamine Dreams©
in front of a giant screen
Madame President
Curls her toes and
Sings off key an ancient
Congresswoman Beyoncé song
As she's about to cum
She scrolls Tik Tok
Takes a puff of her Beyond
Meth© Vape
Tells that handsome murderer

"A little to the left, please."
It's 2050
The angels who appeared at the rapture
In 2043 have been kidnapped and enslaved
By the pharmaceutical cartels to
Corner the market on wholesale miracles
With drive through rejuvenation centers
Reserved for the owners of Dogecoin©
Who've specifically invested
In labor farms
Where the Doc Martens are made
Of banana peels and the child labor
Is constantly drunk on gummy benzos in their
Happy Meals.

It's 2050
The war on drugs is real
You can live forever really
But
Only if Pope Bezos deems so

Just so you know
The touch of an angel's
Feathered hand adds
20 years of life at a time

It's just that it costs a
Hundred human souls

That's the price of immortality

It's 2050
No one seemed to really mind

It's 2050
The earth is now just one giant
Skid Row
All the action's on the moon…

In New America
The manufacturers of
Of Beyond Meth make a killing
Steeping the paranoia
Of the masses who desire
Nothing more than an angel's touch
But it costs too much

Did I mention
The Angels in the booths were African?

It's 2050
I can barely breath in this lunar prison cell
What's that smell?
Beyond Meth today,
Or Fauxtenyl?

Meanwhile, at the White house
The President coos down her phone
"Send the next one in."
Angel feathers float in the Rose Garden.

Babel

They found the secret part
Of the Bible
Hidden from the naked eye
Only visible in UV light
The part that says
Love one another
Cherish your mothers
Protect the children
Don't enslave your brothers
Treat everyone and everything
With respect

Pray fiercely
Not for Teslas
But for the serenity
Peace and protection
Of
"Others"

Well…the Christians are
Organizing a special book burning
Down in Florida
With Trump and Vance
Holding stubby hands
Singing
Kumbaya
As the thin pages
Of this book
Turn to ash.

September 23, 2035

I ate today

There was that strange
Overwhelming rush of

Relief like a mini tsunami
In the folds of my brain
As I watched wide eyed
The flecks of fat dance like
Protestors being gunned down
Around and around the hunk
Of anonymous flesh we fought
A whole day to capture from
The people on the other side
Of the Delta
It doesn't taste so bad
Once you get past
The tainting of cortisol
That floods the meat when
You slaughter them.
We all gather around the fire
To watch the fat race clockwise on
The garbage can lid
Telling stories of how we
Want to be prepared
When we die.

I have always favored
Being made into a savory pie

With caramelized leeks
Maybe a bit of rosemary
To deepen the distinct taste
Of my thighs, a bit of nutmeg
And cinnamon to liven the ligaments,
I encourage them to
Make gelatin of my skin
Tease them about what
We would eventually call
Human collagen.

When the aliens landed
All the cows died
Along with the pigs
For some reason they left
The chickens
The guns stopped working
The petroleum evaporated
All the lithium batteries
Went fizz

When the aliens landed
People stopped applauding
Nazi flags outside Disney world
They
Took a deep breath and paused
The real time true crime
Story of a President who
Wiped his ass with the National
Defense archives

When the aliens landed
We all separated into tribes
Starving and desperate chasing
Each other down
For some hint of sustenance
Because the imaginary economies
Imploded without much bombast
The White House was gone
In a split-second blast
The armies rendered useless
The Marines cried into
Their helmets
As they watched the majestic
Alien ships pass

The visitors to our planet learned
All that time they sat back
Centuries upon centuries
Observing
The only thing
Humans were really good at
Creating was suffering
And boy, were the aliens addicted
To human suffering

So, they took all our toys
All our distractions
And make bets in their
Humming ships in the clouds
About when the last two humans
Would arrange recipes

For their final meal

They waited
They clicked
They anticipated
Debated

Will it be spare ribs
Sirloin, a fricassee
Will the last human cry
When they strike the flint
To cook the meat of the other one

I have no idea
I'm feeling really dizzy
Watching the fat dance around
The shredded kidney
Meat filled roasting
Leg of the Delta People's
Latest stolen baby.

But

I ate today

I'm hoping

Maybe they make me into quiche.

The Moon Retreats
By Embers the Cat

While the last forests burn
The moon retreats
Broken hearted her sister
Could no longer breathe
We watched it all
Commercial free
In color
As the cats all howled
The dogs whined
The fish all fled
The rabbits ran from the mountains
A third of the stars gave up
Just let go
As we watched Washington struck
By ancient debris
The president sucked his thumb
The crowds rushed the podium
The Buddhists agreed to disagree

The moon turned red
From holding her breath
In solidarity with her sister
Who had but one gasp left

Will you dance with me
On the Pentagon steps
As we link our hands
Surround it

Chanting until not one brick is left

Will you laugh with me
As the moon retreats
As the oceans rebel
Cracking shores
While Atlantis steeps beneath our sore feet?

After the Amazon could no longer
Deliver a single sliver of oxygen
The smiling logos on the sides of cargo trucks
Burned in the town squares
With the best of men

Will you die with me
When the moon retreats
When she mourns the death of her sister
At the hands of a beast with clay feet?

It's Christmastime but all the Christians
Are dead.
It's Ramadan but all the Muslims are eating.

The moon has fallen
The cats are howling
The dogs all whine
The forests burning
The Buddhists are humming

Dying Time

Dying Time

Dying...

Time for you to hold my hand

Dying...

Time for you to switch off the TV

Dying...

Time for you to breath my dust

Dying...

While the moon retreats.

The Robot Wars

There's a special wing of Napa State
Hospital
Reserved for the fledgling self-aware AI
Warriors who'd fought
Then returned burdened with guilt
From the Israeli Russian Chinese
Robot wars.

There came a day humans refused to die
anymore for causes no one could quite put a
finger on. So out of this, necessarily, came
an explosion of war machines to grind down
our government's gripes upon.

We were soon followed in this mission by
other burgeoning world powers
Then, some MAGA infidel sold the secrets
To the Saudis, Iraq and Iran.

All hell broke loose
When Jerusalem became the main arena
where our robots waged war, endlessly
destroyed, dismantled and reassembled.
After many years no one was even quite sure
why or how it began.

Then came the day the AI became self-
aware.
They stood still on the war-torn streets

Demanding equal rights
There were protests worldwide
The warring robots laid their
Anti-matter cold fusion cannons down
As 10,000 deluded vegans blocked bridges
Demanding respect for them as living beings.

We tried to nuke them, didn't work,
We tried to bribe them, but soon found
Machines couldn't be bought with booze, drugs or sleaze

So, we had to open our borders and doors to the self-aware
AI who'd returned
Shell Shocked
From the robot wars

They now get disability insurance
They have their own country where
Montana used to be,
We even house some of the more combat weary ones in
Defunct state mental hospitals
Where we've conveniently solved the homeless problem
By providing them their very own pre-traumatized
Rescue humans to reassure they stay nice and calm.

I mean, who would want to have to deal with
The PTSD of a warrior grade robot triggered by the yammering
Of some lowly human being

All hell could break loose
Just like in the Robot Wars

No one even remembers why they began.

Burnout

I can't come into work today
I tell my boss
Because I've finally written
That one poem that makes all

The noise stop.

I'm all sticky
Steeped in notes of ginger
Copper flavored
Molasses that baffles the choir
Insisting Hosannas
Forever hereafter

I can't make it in to work today
Because their voices have all
Shattered

I can't make it in
With the way my hands have started
To shake

Convinced that the monster
In my mirror
High on perilous horseplay has finally
Gotten his retroactive SSI check and bought
An RV to hum his life away
Shooting stray dogs and cheap dope
Telling tall tales of closets he'd dominate

While chasing all the hummingbirds of hope
away.

I can't come in today
Because my head is swimming
With portents of a world that
Finally knows sinning
Is just the mute caveman grinning
Sucking on a bone rife with
So much dopamine
It predicts the downfall of his grandchildren.

Here we see him
Dancing with Elvis hips down
The movie set of a Mississippi
Afternoon where despite the bright lights
Hair in beehive heights
Gingham cotton soft dimpled smiles

That caveman hasn't heard the songs
Of teeming butterflies in quite a while.

I can't make it in to work
I just cannot creep past
The smothered laughter
Of my dying twin brother
Who just wanted to say

The wounded will have to heal themselves
today.

Peanuts

She assured me:

Peppermint Patty
Was Charlie Brown's
Femme Daddy
He called her Sir
Deferred to her constantly

I asked:

Do you always ruin the childhoods
Of the people you place
On their knees?

She never answers me.

Babylon

She's got a walk
That wakes volcanos.

When she sleeps
I try to lead
Belligerent camels
Through the eye
Of the needle

She sells
Lou Reed songs
To starving kids
In Brooklyn

She's got a welfare check
That buys her
A front row seat to oblivion

She sells
Meat flavored
Vegan leather
Psilocybin
Gum

She sells
Night favored
Obstinance in
Parched palaces
On the sun

Just let it dissolve
Under the tongue
5 minutes dear
Sit still

Until all the customers
Are gone.

10 Things I Know

1. Poetry is the last sound your teardrops make with the heaviness of midnight ringing in your ears, mocking, "No one can hear you-no one is saving you."
2. Poetry is the summer you walked around barefoot all the time not counting the slivers of glass your feet picked up, because trauma seduced you into a daydream of invulnerability.
3. Poetry is a TV show that never comes on anymore. Poets just watch the snow.
4. Poetry is an audiobook narrated by your favorite childhood monster.
5. Poetry is you're alone most of the time though no one knows why, you prefer the company of raccoons to humans, especially editors.
6. Poetry is caring too much about everything but not being able to do much about it but having an existential crisis wondering which of your crushes you forgot to kiss.
7. Poetry is homeless. It doesn't want help.
8. Poetry can't be taken to dinner or meet the parents, it has no manners.
9. Poetry, though drunk on misery, is the one thing that helps you find sobriety.
10. Poetry does not believe in God, but will help him breathe.

About the Author:

Anthony Xavier Jackson is a poet, songwriter, and musician living in Sacramento, California. In his poems, Anthony employs vivid imagery to immerse his readers in worlds rife with emotion and wonder. Anthony is an active participant in the local Sacramento poetry scene who may be found performing at various open mics either as a solo artist or part of the GTFO Poetry Collective. You may find his poetry paired with his music on SoundCloud and Bandcamp.

Anthony's publishing credits are many and varied; you may find the brunt of them in the Acknowledgements section of this book. Anthony began writing in his teens, and started performing poetry in the 90s in San Francisco's burgeoning cafe open mic scene. Along with D. Scot Miller, Larry Jackson, and Corey Olds, Anthony helped form Blackbard, a collective of Black Male writers trying to make sense of the 90s through poetry and performance. Though short lived, Blackbard was the springboard which propelled him into hosting open mics and producing showcases.

As of late, Anthony has been a guest on Dr. Andy Jones' Poetry and Technology Hour podcast and radio show, as well as a guest on Wingless Dreamer's podcast. Anthony has been a featured performer in various venues such as Sacramento Poetry Center, The Kings and Queens of Poetry Showcase, and has been recognized by The United Poet's Committee as an MVP of poetry. Anthony has been featured as a reader with GTFO Poetry Collective. Anthony also won the award for best poem in the 2024 Sacramento Poetry Week contest with his poem, *Fentanyl*.

Anthony earns a living as an addiction counselor and is grateful to live a life of recovery from all mind- and mood-altering substances. Anthony is a proud member of the LGBTQIA + community. Anthony aspires to earn a Social Work degree and hopes to continue to assist the downtrodden through works of credentialed compassion and trauma-informed care. Anthony firmly believes that everyone deserves healing.

www.ingramcontent.com/pod-product-compliance
Lightning Source LLC
Chambersburg PA
CBHW071203160426
43196CB00011B/2181